Wen Ma
Shanlin Tzu

NEWLY REVISED QINGJING JING AND YINFU JING

Wen Ma
Shanlin Tzu

NEWLY REVISED QINGJING JING AND YINFU JING

By Shanlin-Tzu 山林子

JustFiction Edition

Imprint

Any brand names and product names mentioned in this book are subject to trademark, brand or patent protection and are trademarks or registered trademarks of their respective holders. The use of brand names, product names, common names, trade names, product descriptions etc. even without a particular marking in this work is in no way to be construed to mean that such names may be regarded as unrestricted in respect of trademark and brand protection legislation and could thus be used by anyone.

Cover image: www.ingimage.com

Publisher:
JustFiction! Edition
is a trademark of
Dodo Books Indian Ocean Ltd. and OmniScriptum S.R.L publishing group

120 High Road, East Finchley, London, N2 9ED, United Kingdom
Str. Armeneasca 28/1, office 1, Chisinau MD-2012, Republic of Moldova, Europe
Printed at: see last page
ISBN: 978-620-0-10552-3

TO MY PARENTS

Moral wisdom is Power, Humankind is Calling for Moral Wisdom Education!

"Moral wisdom education" should be an issue that concerns and is stressed by all humankind. However, few people today pay attention to it, especially the youths in the current society. Young people often believe that it is a matter of concern with thinkers, philosophers and educationists, and has nothing to do with themselves.

Humankind's experience proves a nation that lacks in moral wisdom education is a nation without a future! A nation that lacks in moral wisdom education is a nation without hope!

The root of a nation and the soul of a nation are all grounded in moral wisdom education. Our nation has always been known for emphasizing moral wisdom education.

Moral wisdom education improves people's life quality and life style. Moral wisdom education guides people to attain moral wisdom. Moral wisdom education respects humankind's moral wisdom as a life spirit. The nature of moral wisdom education is to fundamentally enhance people's heart-and-body quality. Moral wisdom education will ultimately help people truly understand the very reason for moral wisdom in the natural lives of humankind.

The number of talented persons with moral wisdom determines the overall quality of a nation and its people, as well as the developmental direction for fields such as science, education and so on.

Where do talented persons with moral wisdom come from? They only come from moral wisdom education. The ultimate goal of moral wisdom education is to cultivate a large number of talented persons with moral wisdom for the nation and the society of humankind. These talented persons are equipped with qualifications of moral wisdom. They are self-innovative, self-creative and harmonious in heart and body. Moral wisdom education will inevitably change the future destiny of humankind.

Currently, the problems due to the absence of moral wisdom education has led to inharmonious phenomenon occurring in our society. Many people have high intelligence but low moral wisdom. The severe imbalance between intelligence and moral wisdom has caused many conflicting phenomena happening in our society. As far as I am concerned, the existence of these conflicts is a result of human problems. Fundamentally, it is a problem of people's moral wisdom. Therefore, failure to solve the problem of moral wisdom education will greatly impact the future progress and development of the whole humankind and each individual.

Currently, a large number of wise people have already realized the significance of the issue concerning moral wisdom education and have begun to advocate that education shall start with self-moral-wisdom-education. People shall autonomously discover their moral wisdom, autonomously master their moral wisdom, and autonomously apply their moral wisdom. It is only when these actions are taken that people will transform themselves to become the ones with moral wisdom and will use moral wisdom to think, to speak and do things. In other words, they will survive in accordance with moral wisdom. It is only when every individual accepts moral wisdom education that all types of society with ideological diversity, all groups of people with language diversity, and all individuals will be able to possess and sustain a natural, harmonious and happy status - a status of moral wisdom.

Each one of us is equipped with moral wisdom. The only difference dwells in the level of discovery. As the theory of gold hiding underneath the ground indicates, without discovery and without mining, gold will not emerge by itself. Similarly, moral wisdom is within each individual. It waits for each individual her/himself to autonomously discover, autonomously master, and autonomously apply. Thus, each person can autonomously discover moral wisdom, each person can autonomously master moral wisdom, and each person can autonomously apply moral wisdom in life practices.

Throughout human history, many thinkers, philosophers, educationists, artists and scientists have always autonomously discovered and autonomously master moral wisdom, and have always autonomously applied moral wisdom to explore moral wisdom education. Evidences show that, it is only through moral wisdom education, hundreds and thousands of autonomously innovative and talented persons with moral wisdom can be created for a society. It is moral wisdom that created the prime artist Leonardo da Vinci in the Western land; it is moral wisdom that created the great thinker and educationist Confucius in Chinese history; and it is moral wisdom that created the scientist and inventor Thomas Edison, who did not own school credentials, but possessed moral wisdom.

Moral wisdom education embraces like sky's broadness, earth's profundity, and nature's simplicity; Moral wisdom education represents humankind's natural characters and their abilities to challenge the conventional way of thinking; moral wisdom educationunderstands that genuine love is a great love of moral wisdom,which bestows the very reason for human existence; moral wisdom education is the magic that lets us to not hold on to hardship, but to use the sword of moral wisdom   to conquer any difficulties.

In the contemporary world, how many teachers and parents pay attention to moral wisdom education? Some teachers and parents seem to forget about how they spent their childhood. In my perspective, as the main subjects of moral wisdom education, it is not the time to teach children moral wisdom before teachers and parents discover their own moral wisdom, because a lot of things in their minds that are considered to be correct have not yet been approved as truth. Thus, we must never force children to do things that they do not want to do, nor force them to do things or work that are favoured by teachers and parents themselves. Research results indicate that one of the main reasons of why children have lost their moral wisdom is due to the absence of teachers' and parents' moral wisdom. How could they inspire children's moral wisdom? Their so-called education philosophy is like a gardener who lost her/his moral wisdom: using their own likenesses and perceptions to twist the little tree that is growing as straight as possible into the shape of an S. They show and tell their products to others: it is my carefully cultivated arts. Therefore, I advise to parents and teachers: in terms of nurturing and educating children, before your discovery and mastery of moral wisdom do not make the same mistake as the gardener. Of course, here I have a simple and convenient method that parents and teachers might want to give a try. If you expect children to develop good habits, then teachers and parents shall foremost develop good habits; if you expect to cultivate a responsible child, then teachers and parents shall foremost cultivate themsevles to be responsible; if you expect to cultivate a confident child, then parents and teachers shall foremost cultivate themsevles to be confident; if you expect to cultivate a child possessing moral wisdom, then teachers and parents shall foremost own moral wisdom. In other words, example of moral wisdom is better than rigid percept.

Moral wisdom is the everlasting existence of origin. It does not differ among nationalities, ethnic groups, or between you and I, home and aboard. As long as we are not interfered by cognition, emotion and will, moral wisdom can be seen in all places. Each one of us shall apply moral wisdom to engage in self-education. When a person truly discover sone's own moral wisdom, she/he will be able to applying moral wisdom to educate her/himself, and will be able to reflect on her/his own life journey. The key here is proper guidance and education. As far as I am concerned, the most advanced, practical and economical educational method is applying moral wisdom to self-educate and becoming a person with moral wisdom. When moral wisdom is mastered, teachers and parents will no longer experience confusion and pain; or engage in extreme behaviours due to the absence of moral wisdom, such as verbal and physical punishment. On the other hand, teachers and parents with moral wisdom will always follow children's developmental paths, inspire children to discover their own moral wisdom, master their own moral wisdom and apply their own moral wisdom, and guide children to carry out self-education (moral wisdom education).

Education that lacks in moral wisdom is like forcefully locking a bird from the forest into a cage. The little bird will stop eating and will die in a few days. Moral wisdom education teaches us: in the process of education, is it possible for us to take advantage of children's interests to carry out moral wisdom education, and to teach each child to be interested in everything? This way, do we still need to use methods such as verbal and physical punishment or constant reminders during children's learning processes? Isn't the phenomenon of children obsessed with the internet already sending a message to teachers and parents about the significance of interests for children? Thus, moral wisdom education has absolutely nothing to do with the examination-oriented education that teachers and parents are concerned with: post-graduate entrance examination, obtaining certificates, looking for good jobs, and being well ahead of others in the future.

In my opinion, the main responsibility of parents is to provide good care in children's lives: let them eat well, sleep well, dress well and play well. Anything beyond these aspects can be left for the children to handle themselves. Of course, before these acts can be taken, we have to foremost guide and inspire children to enter into the status of moral wisdom.

Engaging in moral wisdom education requires moral wisdom. However, it is not to claim that parents lack moral wisdom. Moral wisdom is within oneself. In everyday life, many parents attend seminars and read books on the topic of parenting to search for the secret recipe of parenting their own child. Yet, how many theories in books can be copied and implemented directly? Experts' seminars are to use their moral wisdom to tell you how to do certain things; parenting knowledge in books illustrates the author's thoughts. The knowledge we learn belongs to others. Why don't you write your own book of parenting? Of course, here we often ignore an important issue: is your child the same as others? Since children are different, how is it possible to use one method to educate your own child? In my opinion, the number of children in the world determines the number of educational methods we shall have. Yet, the general principle cannot be altered. In other words, we must use all types of methods and strategies to guide and to teach children to understand: never lose moral wisdom. The reason why is because the fundamental principle of moral wisdom education is, first of all, to completely abandon all the useless knowledge and personal experience that are stored in one's mind. Then we will be able to discover the wonder of moral wisdom. It is only on the basis of this condition, we will be able to discuss issues of moral wisdom.

As we all know, anything in this world has a principle to follow. Universe and nature has a principle to follow; society has a principle to follow; and life has a principle to follow. It is only when moral wisdom is applied that each person will be able to become truly independent. In are as such as thinking, working and living, each person will be able to reaching to the natural, harmonious and happy status– a status of moral wisdom.

The nature of engaging in moral wisdom fundamentally enhances people's heart-and body quality. Moral wisdom education will ultimately teach us to understand the authentic meaning of human existence. Happiness is a heart-felt experience of moral wisdom. A truthful, good and beautiful heart is bathing under the sunshine of moral wisdom education. They demonstrate the highest aim and excellent realm of moral wisdom education.

Moral wisdom education is an education to enhance life quality and style!

Moral wisdom education is an education to guide people to attain moral wisdom education!

Moral wisdom education is an education to respect people's morally wise life spirit.

Friends, for the establishment of a community of shared future for humankind, and the fulfillment of the dream of the world for a path of peaceful development, let us hold hands together to carry out moral wisdom education that is filled with naturalness, harmony and happiness!

Moral wisdom is power, humankind is calling for moral wisdom education!

THE NEWLY REVISED QINGJING JING
(An educational poem of natural wisdom)

Without a body, the nature creates the Dao and De;
Without a print, the Dao and De apply wisdom and intelligence;
Without a form, wisdom and intelligence regulate the course of the universe;
Without feelings, the universe raises and nourishes the lively myriad beings.

自然无体兮化用道德

道德无迹兮能用慧智

慧智无形兮相显乾坤

乾坤无情兮万物生机

The wisdom of the sky and earth can be pure or turbid, moving or tranquil;
The sky is pure and moving, and the earth is turbid and tranquil;
The male is pure and moving, and the female is turbid and tranquil;
Purity: the source of turbidity; movement: the root of tranquility.

天地德慧兮清浊动静

天清地浊兮天动地静

男清女浊兮男动女静

清者浊源兮动者基静

When humans are pure and tranquil, the sky and earth will return to their
natural states;
Originally, human nature is pure; yet, senses stir up confusion;
In the beginning, human mind is tranquil; yet illusive desires act in a wild way;
It is only to distinguish illusive desires, a person's nature will be tranquil and
mind will be calm.

人能清静兮回归自然

人性本清兮而意识乱

人心本静兮而妄欲猖

能灭妄欲兮性静心安

When a person's nature is tranquil and mind is calm, his expenditure, anger and
foolishness will be destroyed;
Before wisdom appears, one will find it hard to distinguish his illusive desires;
He who gets rid of illusive desires makes his mind and nature bright;
His nature is without a type, and mind without a course.

性心静安兮贪嗔痴灭

妄欲难除兮慧智未启

能灭妄欲兮明心见性

性无其性兮心无其踪

When a person's nature, mind and images are without forms, what he sees:
nothingness;
When the three entities become nothingness, one's body turns empty;
When the body of image turns empty, he observes nothingness in all emptiness;
In all emptiness, one observes nothing; he reaches nothingness and the middle
of the way.

性心形无兮唯见於无

三者既空兮一体相空

一体亦空兮空所空无

所空既无兮无无中中

In the condition of nothingness and the middle of the way, a person reaches the
state of restfulness;
When his restfulness is without an image of restfulness, how could his illusive
desires rise?
When his illusive desires cannot rise, his mind is truly tranquil and nature
regulated to rest;
When truth and regulation return, his body and its application are the same.

无无中中兮湛然常寂

寂无所寂兮妄欲焉生

妄欲不生兮真寂常静

真常回归兮体用相同

When responding things with a tranquil mind, a person dwells upon a tranquil realm;
When arriving in a tranquil realm, a true being will be pure and tranquil;
A pure and tranquil being of truth shall bring moral and virtues in oneness;
When moral and virtues are in oneness, the Way is brought about.

寂静应物兮寂静性境

性境常应兮真人清静

清静真人兮道德合一

道德合一兮名为道成

Although by name, the Way is a triumph; yet, nothing is fulfilled;
It is only for the act of enlightening humans, the Way is given a false name;
If one is able to distinguish illusive desires, his moral wisdom will illustrate
itself;
When his moral wisdom illustrates itself, how could he not become a sage or
an exemplary person?

虽名道成兮实无所成

启迪众生兮假道虚名

能灭妄欲兮德慧自显

德慧自显兮焉非贤圣

A wise person has no contentions, yet a foolish one is fond of it;
Moral wisdom is without morals; he who holds fast morals when his morals
covered with haze;
When a person holds fast his moral and virtues, his moral and virtues are not
real;
When all the living grieves over morals, illusive desires lead them doubt.

慧智无争兮愚痴好争

德慧不德兮慧霾执德

执著道德兮道德非真

众生悯德兮妄欲致惑

When illusive desires exist, the Way of a person will be darkening;
When the Way of a person is darkening, he will grieve his morals;
When a person grieves his morals, he will cut off his wisdom;
When a person cuts of his wisdom, he will leave his intelligence perplexed.

既有妄欲兮必霾其道

既霾其道兮必惘其德

既惘其德兮必断其慧

既断其慧兮必迷其智

When the intelligence of a person perplexed, he will be captivated by all living
things;
When a person is captivated by all living things, he will indulge in the pursuit
of them;
When a person indulges in the pursuit of them, he will bring forth worries;
When a person brings forth worries, his mind and body will be shackled.

既迷其智兮必著万物

既著万物兮必生贪恋

既生贪恋兮必生烦恼

既生烦恼兮心身枷监

When a person's mind and body shacked, his mind suffers and body is ill;
Fame, profit, power and women will lead him drift about in the sea of life and
death;
When one will sink into an abyss of misery, his naturalness will be forever lost;
When one can enlighten naturalness, his purity and tranquility will always
remain.

心枷身监兮心苦身病

名利贵色兮流浪死生

常沉苦海兮永失自然

得悟自然兮常清常静

THE NEWLY REVISED HUANGDI YINFU JING
(An educational poem of natural moral wisdom)

PREFACE

Yin: its body is silent, its acts are void, and there is no image to trace;
Fu: its flow and motion are in oneness; the body of sameness has no splits;
Jing; natural morals; its rules cannot be violated;
Natural moral wisdom: the tool to revolve the Yin and Fu;
It is so void that it is pure, tranquil, simple, and has no illusive deeds;
It creates the sky, earth, creatures, and humans with relaxing bend and stretch;
Tai chi, Yin and Yang, gathering and disperse: the nature of movement and tranquility;
The wonder of sky, earth, creature and humans is revealed by the scripture of Yin Fu.

序

阴者体默用虚兮无相可寻

符者同运同行兮同体不分

经者自然道德兮律不能背

自然道德慧智兮阴符器运

虚无纯粹易简兮清静无为

造化天地物人兮张弛曲伸

太极阴阳聚散兮动静气质

天地物人妙秘兮阴符泄尽

CHAPTER ONE

If one observes moral and virtues of naturalness, all that its wise practice is
natural;
The sky, earth, creature and humans: who can live about without it?
To the sky, earth, creature and humans there belong the five (mutual) elements,
and the image of their use and the root of their bodies;
To distinguish illusive desires and illustrate wisdom are sage and exemplary
persons who naturally comply.

第一章

观自然之道德兮自然慧行

天地万物人类兮离之谁能

天地物人五运兮用相根体

灭妄显慧圣贤兮自然顺应

The same five elements are in the mind and body of man, and their roots are
tied with moral and virtues;
The sky and earth are at one's disposal, and all things receive their
transformations from the mind and body;
Moral wisdom is human origin setting a person's mind, nature, body and fate;
When one can enlighten the Dao, understand reasons, and know himself, a true
person is thereby determined.

五运存乎心身兮根系道德

天地存乎一掌兮造化心身

道德慧智人本兮心性身命

明道懂理知己兮修养真人

When moral wisdom moves the sky, the stars and constellations lie hidden in
darkness;
When moral wisdom moves the earth, multiple beings appear on the ground;
When moral wisdom moves humans, life is put to living and death;
When the sky, earth, creature and humans exert their powers in concert, all
transformations have their commencements determined.

道德慧运天穹兮移星易辰

道德慧运大地兮万物生机

道德慧运人类兮性命冲和

天地物人同运兮万化定基

Moral wisdom, intelligence and feelings are in the three most important
movements and restfulness;
When fire of Yang arises in wood of Yin, the Yang is sure to go on to the
destruction of the Yin;
When calamity arises in a state, the Yin is sure to go on to the destruction of
the Yang;
When one enlightens the Dao, understands reasons, and carries out rightful

conduct, the sage teaches thousands of generations.

德慧智知情意兮三要动静

阳火生于阴水兮阳兴阴衰

奸佞藏于家国兮阴强阳弱

明道懂理正行兮圣教万代

CHAPTER TWO

When the wisdom of Spring and autumn revolves, Spring leaves, autumn
meets;
Nature, morals and wise reasoning: the rules of these three Powers are the
same;
The mother of the sky, earth and creations are the mother of all things;
To give birth or subdue, to limit or widen, and to balance: the sky and earth are
brought forth.

第二章

春秋德慧交替兮春散秋聚

自然道德慧理兮三才律同

天地万物之母兮万物人母

生克制化平衡兮天地共生

During the time of nourishment, all the members are property regulated: the
great medicine of nourishing lives;
When the springs of motion come into play, all transformations quietly take
place;
When humans know the mysteriousness of the Spirit's action, but they do not
enlighten, thus, do not know what is spiritual comes to be so;
When they do not know what is not spiritual comes to be so, their mind suffers
and body is ill.

食其时百骸理兮养生大药

动其机静其妙兮万化安宁

人知其神之神兮不悟不神

不悟不神之神兮心苦身病

The sun and moon have their definite times, and their exact measures are large
and small;
The secrecy of natural moral wisdom cannot be read by foolish ones;
The wonder by which natural moral wisdom holds is invisible and unknown to
all under the sky;
When the superior man has got it, he strengthens his body by it; when the small
man has got it, he makes light of his life.

日月星辰有数兮大小有定

自然道德慧秘兮愚痴无知

自然道德慧妙兮人莫能见

君子得之躬行兮小人鄙视

CHAPTER THREE

The blind hear well, and the deaf see well; to derive all that is advantageous
from one source;
To wisely apply ability that is from one place is a myriad times better;
Fame, profit, power and women are illusive desires and cover one's wisdom
with haze;
Without enlightenment, one wanders around in the world and no regrets eve the
day he ends.

第三章

瞽善听聋善视兮绝利一源

慧能一处智用兮超众万倍

名利贵色妄欲兮幻象霾智

流浪红尘不悟兮至死不悔

Natural morals have no kindness, but so it is that the greatest kindness comes
from it;
The sky, earth, lights, wind and rain all come without its special design;
Perfect motion is the middle way and affability moral wisdom creates;
Perfect stillness is the middle way and correctness of it.

自然道德无恩兮而大恩生

天地光气雨露兮何处不拥

道德慧智至动兮动则中和

道德慧智至静兮静则中中

When moral wisdom seems to be without feelings and desires, it seems to be
most wrapt up in itself;
When moral wisdom is without form and images, its operation is universal in
its character;

It is by its breath that moral wisdom control whatever creature we grasp;

Depending merely ability is to desolate moral wisdom.

德慧无情无意兮情之至私

德慧无形无相兮用之至公

德慧物运以气兮控之以机

只著能力大小兮德慧惘用

Death is the root of life, and life is the root of death;
Kindness springs from injury, and injury springs from kindness;
When a mean person imprisons himself with knowledge, his nature lost and life
in danger;
When an exemplary person enlightens the Dao and understands reasons, he
owns a morally wise mind.

生者死之根蒂兮死者生根

恩宠生于祸害兮害生于恩

小人囚知死识兮迷性惘命

君子明道懂理兮德慧智心

The mean person by studying the phenomena and laws of sky and earth
becomes sage;
The wise person by enlightening the Dao, understanding reasons and knowing
oneself becomes tact;
The mean person is perplexed about the foolishness of sages who profit others
at the expense of themselves;
The wise person follows the lead of the wise sages who have a proper stance
and walk on the path of rightful conduct.

知晓天文地理兮愚称渊博

明道懂理知己兮智称圆通

愚称虞舜愚钝兮损己利他

智效虞舜慧智兮定位正行

Sages enlighten the Dao when they observing the four seasons rotate in the sky;
Exemplary persons understand reasons when noticing the multiple things produce on earth;
Humans who situate themselves in the middle of the sky and earth go through life and death;
Cultivating himself, regulating his families and governing his state: a man examines himself at all times.

天运四时变化兮圣人明道

地运万物生长兮贤人理明

人居天地之中兮造化生死

修身齐家治国兮六时常省

The method of moral wisdom proceeds in stillness, and so it was that the sky,
earth, and all things were produced;
The wisdom of the sky and earth proceeds gently and gradually, and thus it is
that the Yin and Yang adapt;
The one takes the place of the other and change proceeds: they arrive or leave;
oppose or submit;
When the sky, earth and multiple creations take their proper stances, they will
act in a natural way.

自然道德至静兮天地物生

天地慧智至微兮阴阳变通

阴阳相推变化兮聚散逆顺

天地万物定位兮自然运行

Sages enlighten the Dao, understand reasons and comply with naturalness;
They distinguish illusive desires, reveal moral wisdom, reach the way of
perfect stillness, and unite with the Dao;
The book of He, Luo, the eight diagrams, and the sexagenary cycle: they
classify and represent the sky and earth;
The five-system and the nine-numbers belonging to the sky imitate the earth:
they are the Spirit-like springs of power.

圣人明道懂理兮顺应自然

灭妄欲显德慧兮致静合道

河洛八卦甲子兮类象天地

五体天九法地兮神藏机妙

China's culture and civilization has been transmitted in an uninterrupted flow;
The root of Fuxi and the pulse of Huangdi will alive without an end;
The reviving of China conforms to the sky and earth;
To build a unified world is the duty to which we are called upon.

华夏文明文化兮源远流长

根伏羲脉黄帝兮万古不亡

中华民族复兴兮顺天应地

构建世界大同兮当仁不让

I want morebooks!

Buy your books fast and straightforward online - at one of world's fastest growing online book stores! Environmentally sound due to Print-on-Demand technologies.

Buy your books online at
www.morebooks.shop

Kaufen Sie Ihre Bücher schnell und unkompliziert online – auf einer der am schnellsten wachsenden Buchhandelsplattformen weltweit! Dank Print-On-Demand umwelt- und ressourcenschonend produzi ert.

Bücher schneller online kaufen
www.morebooks.shop

info@omniscriptum.com
www.omniscriptum.com

Printed by Books on Demand GmbH, Norderstedt / Germany